What Lives in the Garden?

John Woodward

SCHOLASTIC INC.

New York Toronto London Auckland Sydney
Mexico City New Delhi Hong Kong Buenos Aires

ISBN 0-439-65546-3

Copyright © 2000 by Haldane Mason Ltd. All rights reserved.
Published by Scholastic Inc., 557 Broadway, New York, NY 10012,
by arrangement with Barron's Educational Series, Inc.
SCHOLASTIC and associated logos are trademarks
and/or registered trademarks of Scholastic Inc.

12 11 10 9 8 7 6 5 4 3   4 5 6 7 8 9/0

Printed in the U.S.A.   40

First Scholastic printing, March 2004

Editors: Ben Keith, Beck Ward

Designer: Phil Ford

Picture Research: Ben Keith

Picture Acknowledgments

Bruce Coleman Collection: /M.P.L. Fogden 11; /Jen & Des Bartlett 25t; /Jon Cancalosi 25b;
Holt Studios International: /Nigel Cattlin 39t; **Natural History Museum:** 12;
NHPA: /N. Callow 8b, 14, 17t, 26, 40t; /Martin Garwood 15t, 16t 21t; /Martin Wendler 21b; /G.I. Bernard 22; /A.N.T. 24r;
/Richard Knightbridge 30; /Dr Eckart Pott 38; /Daniel Heuclin 33; /Stephen Dalton 8r, 17b, 20b, 24b; /Dan Griggs 39;
Oxford Scientific Films: /Jorge Sierra 8t; /Mantis Wildlife Films 16b, 40b; /G.A. Maclean 18; /John Cheverton 31t;
~/David G. Fox 20t; /Jim Bockowski 41t; /Breck P. Kent 41b; **Premaphotos Wildlife:** /Ken Preston-Mafham 24t;
Science Photo Library: /Andrew Syred 6, 29, 32; /Eye of Science 4, 42; /Claude Nuridsany & Marie Perennou 5, 7, 10l, 13b, 23, 28, 35–7;
/Dr Jeremy Burgess 9, 15b, 31b, 43t; /Dr John Brackenbury 13t; /Simone D. Pollard 27t; /Sinclair Stammers 34; /David Scharf 19;
/Dr Morley Read 43b.

Contents

Introduction

Some of the most fascinating animals in the world live just a few steps from your back door. You don't have to go to the African plains or the Amazon rainforests – just step outside and take a walk down your garden path.

If it's summer, the place will be literally buzzing with bees on the flowers, grasshoppers chirping in the grass, and hoverflies humming through the air.

This orb-web spider waits patiently for its insect prey.

It's a jungle out there!

Once you start looking, you'll discover more and more. You'll see spiders building their wonderful webs or stalking their victims, ants tending flocks of aphids, and nasty-looking insects crawling from the pond and transforming themselves into jeweled dragonflies. It's magical!

A garden is a like a miniature nature reserve for tiny creatures. You may get a few bigger ones in it as well, but they tend to stay well hidden. Insects and their leggy friends – and enemies – are not so shy. They carry on with their lives whether you are there or not, and it's great to watch them. And who knows? They may be watching you, too!

Untidy paradise

Some gardens are better for small animals than others. Big, old gardens that have gone wild are best because they provide many places to live and plants to feed on. Most gardens are not like this, of course, but they do sometimes have wild corners, handy heaps of dead leaves, or comfortable piles of logs for small creatures to live in.

Blackflies like to suck blood, so beware!

Killer spray

Some garden animals are pests – they eat the plants, and some may bite or sting. A few may even be dangerous. Many people think that the garden is better off without them and spray poisonous chemicals on the plants, hoping to kill these tiny creatures. Sometimes this works, but then more pests usually come along. The plants have to be sprayed again, and the poison kills all the other small creatures as well, including the ones that eat the pests. Eventually, most of the insects disappear, along with the spiders and birds that prey upon them, and the garden just isn't the same. So let them live.

What Lives in the Grass?

Most backyards have a patch of grass or even a prize-winning lawn that looks and feels like a green carpet. More probably, though, it is a bumpy playground full of bikes and barbecues. In the city, it is usually next to another yard, but out of town the grass is often just an extension of a half-wild meadow, road verge or railway embankment. If they get the chance, the creatures that live out on the rough grassland will slip through the fence and move into your yard.

Often they don't get much of a chance, because lawns usually get mowed once a week or so. But in areas beneath trees and fences, the grass can grow tall, forming a miniature jungle and offering food and shelter to all kinds of climbing and burrowing insects – and the spiders and other killers that eat them.

Songs of summer

What would summer be without grasshoppers? These noisy insects love wide stretches of long grass, where they use their tough biting jaws to eat the grass blades. Male grasshoppers make their chirpy songs by rubbing a row of pegs on the inside of each long back leg against the toughened edge of a folded wing. Some females can sing too, but usually not as loudly.

Male grasshoppers sing to attract females.

Highjumpers

If you get too close to a grasshopper, it will fall silent and leap away, catapulting itself into the air with its power-packed hind legs. Many grasshoppers can also fly, suddenly opening a set of dazzlingly bright hind wings. When they land, they hide their colored wings and disappear, like sparks blinking out. It's a clever way of confusing enemies, and it certainly confuses us too!

Locust plague

The locusts that plague desert areas are really just big grasshoppers. If rain transforms their desert into a green oasis, they multiply so fast that they eat every plant in the area. They fly off in search of more food – in vast swarms of up to 50 billion insects! Locusts can descend on unsuspecting fields and consume a whole farm's crops within hours, and a big swarm could even wreck a whole nation's economy.

This adult desert locust can strip a plant in minutes.

Megaphone

The grasshopper's song is just a rasping buzz, but some crickets make really musical sounds. The field cricket is a shiny black beast that sings near the entrance to its burrow down in the grass. The champion singer is the burly, burrowing *mole cricket*, who digs a trumpet-shaped burrow to amplify its song like a megaphone. On summer evenings, you can hear its deep, soft chirping from up to a mile away!

The burly back legs of a grasshopper are designed for a fast getaway.

Eerie glow

While some insects sing to attract mates, others glow. Long grass sometimes contains female glow-worms, which climb the stems at dusk to flash their valentine messages into the summer night. Each glow-worm is a wingless beetle equipped with light organs in her tail. These glow with an eerie yellow-green light when oxygen combines with a protein called luciferin and an enzyme called luciferase. The light organs are connected to special air tubes to ensure they get a good oxygen supply, so by opening and closing the tubes, the glow-worm can switch herself on and off.

Glow-worms are like night lights for other animals!

BUG ALERT!

Flashpoints

- The glow-worm's chemical lamp is very efficient; 98 percent of the energy is converted into light, not heat – luckily for the glow-worm!
- Tropical fireflies can also produce light and flash coded messages at each other.
- Young glow-worms are voracious predators that attack snails, injecting them with digestive juices that turn the snail's insides into soup.

Furry miners

A few insects live under the lawn. In spring, you may notice small holes appearing on bare patches, each surround by a volcano-like cone of soil grains. These are the burrows of mining bees.

If you watch one of the holes, you may see its builder. She looks like a miniature bumblebee and always lives alone. She lays eggs in her burrow and supplies them with pellets of nectar and pollen gathered from flowers. Then she seals the hole and flies away.

Mining bees like to nest underground.

Busy ants

Ants get everywhere in the yard, but some are particularly busy among the blades of grass. These include harvester ants, which gather the seeds of grasses and other garden plants and carry them back to their nests. They then store them in special chambers where they keep for many weeks. When they need food, they just raid the seed store, just as we might raid the refrigerator.

This black ant defends itself by squirting corrosive acid at an attacker.

Ant wars

Occasionally, an American harvester ant meets its deadly enemy – the fire ant. In the southern states of the U.S., fire ants live in huge colonies. They are tiny yet ferocious, with biting jaws and painful stings, and attack anything that threatens them – even people.

Fire ants often wipe out other types of ants living in the same area, so if a wandering harvester meets a fire ant, it rushes back to its own nest for some reinforcements. The ant armies meet and fight. There is most often wholesale slaughter, and the grass is littered with dead and dying ants.

Secret weapon

Ants also fight battles with termites. There are many kinds of termites. Most eat dead wood, but the harvester termites of the tropics feast on young grass shoots. Harvesters forage for food all around the nest, and often get into gardens.

Termites live in colonies in their millions, looking after one breeding queen. "Worker" termites are easy prey for ants, so heavily-armed soldier termites defend them. Depending on the kind of termite, soldiers may have massive biting jaws or long snouts that squirt sticky, irritating glue, gumming up the attacking ants' jaws.

BUG ALERT!

Living trap

Search in the long grass in any warm country, from southern Europe to Australia, and you may discover a sinister lurking killer – the praying mantis. It's not easy to see, because it disguises itself as a blade of grass to keep hidden from its victims.

A mantis sits and waits, holding its barbed forelegs up as if praying. When an unwary insect strays within range, the mantis watches it intently with spooky eyes, then suddenly snatches the poor insect in a split-second strike. Impaled on those forelegs the insect is helpless as the mantis calmly eats it alive.

Victims of the praying mantis do not feel blessed when they get speared by those forelegs.

Money pit

The purse-web spider lives in a burrow with a lining that extends above ground, just like a silk purse. When an insect walks over the purse, the spider runs up and skewers it through the silk with its extra-long fangs. It cuts a slit in the purse, hauls its victim inside and then sews up the hole.

Is that grass moving, or is it a grass spider?

Mantis morsels

- A mantis can turn its head all the way around, following every move of an unsuspecting approaching victim.
- If it catches a dangerous stinging insect, the praying mantis may kill it by biting off its head.
- The female praying mantis is notorious for eating the male during mating, often snacking on his head.

Megamouth

As you look for a praying mantis, you may see a grass spider. It hides from enemies by stretching its front four legs forward in a bunch, pretending to be part of a grass stem. These spiders have huge jaws and the male uses his to grip the female's fangs during mating to prevent her from eating him.

Big and hairy

The spiders you see most often in the grass are wolf spiders – fast-running hunters that chase their prey instead of trapping it in webs. Some wolf spiders sit in burrows and pounce on passing insects. These home-lovers include a beefy European wolf spider with the scientific name *Lycosa tarantula*. This is the original tarantula, which gave its name to the huge bird-eating spiders of the Americas. You might meet one of these American tarantulas in the southwestern U.S. It's a very different beast from the European wolf spider, though, with long hairy legs, enormous fangs and tiny, virtually useless eyes.

Tarantula tidbits

- American tarantulas can have a legspan of up to 5 inches (13 cm), but some of their relatives from the Amazon, like the goliath bird-eating spider, have a legspan of up to 11 inches (28 cm)!
- These giant spiders really do eat birds if they can catch them, as well as bats and frogs. Mostly, though, they eat big juicy insects such as beetles.
- Tarantulas from the Americas are covered with fine hairs that break easily and puncture your skin like splinters.

BUG ALERT!

Tarantula hawk

It's hard to imagine any insect winning a fight with a tarantula, but there are insects in the American southwest that specialize in hunting these monster spiders. They are called tarantula hawks.

A tarantula hawk is basically a big wasp with a serious sting. She tracks down a tarantula in its burrow and lures it out to fight. As the spider tries to stab the wasp with its fangs, the wasp slips under its guard and plunges in her sting.

A huge hairy spider makes an easy victim for the giant tarantula hawk.

What Visits the Flowers?

Back in the 19th century, intrepid plant hunters explored remote corners of the planet in search of exotic blooms. They brought back thousands of different plants and seeds, and over the years these were crossbred to create plants that never before existed. Most garden flowers have been created in this way.

These plants look great, but they puzzle the wildlife. Their leaves tend to taste all wrong, so most native plant-eating insects steer clear of them. This is good news for gardeners, but it means there are fewer caterpillars and other juicy grubs to attract songbirds. The sugary nectar in their flowers is fine, though, so adult insects fly in to refuel at exotic flowering plants like buddleias. So, while the long grass is home for many creatures, a flower garden is the insect equivalent of a filling station, where most visitors are just passing through.

Iridescent scales

The most conspicuous nectar-feeding insects are butterflies. They live all over the world, and dazzle us with their beauty. Their wonderful wings are big, transparent plates made of plastic-like material called chitin, covered with tiny colored scales arranged like the tiles on a roof. As butterflies get older they lose these scales, and gradually go bald!

Some wing scales reflect light in iridescent blues and purples. Other scales produce fragrances that are irresistible to potential mates. This is just as well, since some butterflies only live for a few weeks – just long enough to mate and lay their eggs.

Butterflies like this tortoiseshell are often more colorful than the flowers they visit.

Whirring wings

At night, when butterflies go to bed, moths come out. They are attracted to plants like honeysuckle, which become more fragrant at night. There are fewer flowers open at night, so the insects go straight from one plant to another.

Butterflies and moths are similar, but they have different flying techniques. While butterflies flap their wings, moths whirr them at high speed. This enables moths to hover like hummingbirds, and one type is actually called the hummingbird hawk moth. Unusually, it flies by day, so you can marvel at it hovering over a flower, inserting its long tongue to drink.

Moths don't get in a flap – they whirr their wings!

Hover power

Hovering nearby may be an insect that looks like a bundle of golden-brown fur with a long pin protruding from the front. This is a bee-fly. It doesn't really hover, though – it clings to the flower with its feet while it drinks with its long proboscis.

The bee-fly is entertaining, but it has a dark secret. It lays its eggs near the nests of mining bees, and when they hatch, the fly maggots crawl into the nests, find the young bees developing inside and slowly eat them alive.

Big mouth strikes again – the bee-fly drinks nectar through its long tubular tongue.

Pollen baskets

The busiest nectar feeders in the flower garden are the honeybees, and with good reason. They live in colonies of 50,000 or more, and all the food for the colony is collected by about half the worker bees. They must feed the other workers, their queen and all the young bee grubs, too.

Nectar is mostly sugar, so to give the growing young a balanced diet, the bees also gather protein-rich pollen. The foraging worker bees carry the pollen back to the hive in pollen baskets on their hind legs. At the hive, they give the pollen and nectar to other bees. These turn the nectar into honey, then store it with the pollen in wax honeycomb cells to feed the colony throughout the winter. It's up to the workers to keep the hive going. No wonder they're so busy!

Their honey may be sweet, but "Africanized" honeybees can be deadly.

Bee business

- When a honeybee finds a good source of nectar, she returns to the hive and lets the other bees know by doing a special dance. The dance tells them how good the nectar is, which way to go, and how far away it is.

- All worker bees in a colony are sisters. They are the sterile daughters of a single breeding female – the queen. They have a few brothers, called drones, but not many. The workers do all the work, including raising a few fertile females that will eventually become queens too.

BUG ALERT!

Killer bees

In Latin America, most of the honeybees have interbred with imported African bees. They are much more fierce than normal bees and if anyone gets too close to their nests, they attack in swarms. Many people die from these attacks every year, so they are known as *killer bees*. They make excellent honey, though.

Furry heavyweights

The most spectacular bees in your yard are big, furry bumblebees. They, too, live in colonies, with many worker bees tending a single queen, but the underground colonies are much smaller and last for just one summer.

Bumblebees feed on nectar and pollen. They have long tongues so they can reach into deep flowers. Some flowers, such as lupins, are made just for bumblebees. They have special spring-loaded landing platforms – when a heavy bumblebee lands on the platform, the flower opens so the bee can get at the nectar. Since smaller, lighter insects cannot do this, the bumblebees know that lupins are unlikely to have been raided already.

Hardworking bumblebees never take a day off.

Death grip

Sometimes a butterfly or bee seems to be sitting strangely still on a flower. If you look more closely, you'll see it is stone dead, impaled on the fangs of an exquisitely camouflaged spider.

The killer is a crab spider. It moves sideways, just like a crab. The most common type is nearly always white, and it likes to sit on the white rays of a daisy, where it is virtually invisible.

The spider's strategy is simple. It sits by a source of nectar and waits, with its front legs held open wide. If an insect settles for a drink, the spider grabs it, then stabs the struggling victim with its fangs, injecting a powerful poison that kills it within seconds. Then, the spider pumps digestive juices into the corpse to liquefy its flesh and sucks it dry.

A hopeful white crab spider tries its luck on a pink flower.

15

Open house

While some flowers are shaped to attract certain insects, others are open to all. They are often alive with flies, bees and small beetles such as rose chafers and soldier beetles, all feeding on the nectar and getting dusted with pollen.

The flowers also attract spider-hunting wasps such as the tarantula hawks, ichneumon wasps, and other predators or parasites. Although these insects feed their young on the flesh of other animals, the adults prefer nectar.

Look closely into the flowers in your garden – this beautiful rose chafer is just one of the hidden delights.

Flowery peril

The crab spider fools its victims because its color exactly matches that of the flower it is sitting on. Some tropical killers go even further and actually look like flowers. One of these is the orchid mantis, a relative of the praying mantis. It is often brightly colored, with flanges and plates on its body that look like the petals of an orchid.

The mantis perches motionless on a stem, its spiked arms held up ready for action. If an insect lands on it, or even flies past, the mantis snatches it up with a lightning movement and devours it.

The ultimate disguise: an orchid mantis.

The little froghopper looks very odd without its foamy disguise.

Cuckoo spit

Check out the soft stems of garden flowers and you'll often find a little blob of foam. Sometimes known as cuckoo spit, this conceals a little green bug called a froghopper.

It is a relative of the greenfly and, as it feeds, it produces a sticky fluid from its back end, blowing air through it to make foam. This soon hides it from its enemies. Some birds have learned that there's a snack beneath the foam, though, so it's not totally foolproof.

Squeak beetle

Some insects in the flower garden have bigger appetites than others. Earwigs may munch through the petals of roses, and bright scarlet lily beetles enrage gardeners by chewing through their prize lilies.

If you try to pick up a lily beetle, it often escapes by dropping to the ground. But if you manage to catch it in your closed hand, it squeaks in protest, hoping you'll drop it in surprise.

Earwigs think nothing of scoffing your prize roses.

What's Buzzing around Your Head?

What could be nicer than lunch in the fresh air, among the flowers and birds? It always seems like a terrific idea, until insects join the feast. Some want to eat your food, like the gangs of stripy wasps that drive people flapping around the lawn. But others want to take a bite out of you – and you may not even notice until bumps appear on your skin the next day.

Striped marauders

Any summer picnic attracts wasps – the yellow-jacketed, stinging wasps that many hoverflies try to imitate. Adult wasps feed their queen's young chewed-up caterpillars, but they prefer something sweeter for themselves. A slice of cake or a juicy peach is a perfect treat. The fact that you might be trying to eat it doesn't bother them. Wave them away and they just come back, time after time. If you do actually hit one, don't be surprised if it stings you.

Just marvel

Some creatures that come buzzing around your head can look alarming, but they are no trouble at all. They are hoverflies – nectar and pollen eating flies that often look just like wasps. Their stripes are a cunning defense trick, since birds are naturally wary of anything that looks as if it might sting.

When a hoverfly lands, you can see it is no wasp. Its eyes are different, with huge honeycomb lenses like those of a blowfly. It also has only two wings instead of four, which improves its flying skill. It can fly forwards, backwards and sideways. It can hover in exactly the same place, and then dart away at such speed that you lose track of it. And if it comes and hovers right in front of your face, don't panic – just marvel.

The hoverfly may look like a wasp, but it's completely harmless.

Bloodsuckers

Wasps are a nuisance, but at least they're only after your lunch. The real villains are mosquitoes, midges and blackflies. These are all two-winged flies, like hoverflies, but with much nastier habits. The females need to eat protein-rich food so they can lay eggs, and one of the richest foods of all is fresh blood.

Mosquitoes and midges are equipped with fine hypodermic needles. They slip them into your skin quite painlessly, so you can be bitten several times before you notice. Blackflies, however, hack at you with their scissor jaws – and they do it in swarms! Such swarms have made some areas of the world almost uninhabitable.

Wasp sandwich

If you're eating outdoors, make sure that any food you're about to bite into doesn't have a wasp on it. The wasp may sting you inside your mouth or throat. The sting then swells up, and apart from being painful, can make it difficult or even impossible to breathe.

BUG ALERT!

Nasty diseases

Bloodsucking is bad enough, but insects also carry diseases. Tropical mosquitoes transmit malaria and yellow fever which kill millions of people every year. Blackflies can carry an infection called river blindness, where thousands of tiny parasitic worms infest the skin and eyes. Together, these bloodsucking flies probably cause more misery than any other creature on Earth.

Blackflies are always on the lookout for a chance to steal some of your blood!

What Lives in the Bushes?

If you go out early on a summer morning, you'll see the bushes festooned with spiderwebs, all silvery with morning dew. They look magical, but just think – each one of those webs is a deadly trap. What must this be like for insects? Imagine living in a city where there is a giant trap at the end of every street, occupied by a man-eating monster. Scary, huh? But it doesn't stop there. There are assassins stalking the leaves of every bush, and muggers lurking in the shadows. There are killers that will lure a male insect to his doom by releasing a scent that imitates the perfume of a courting female. Yet all these hunters can only survive if they have plenty of victims, so a good crop of webs is a sign that your bushes are teeming with life.

The garden spider is almost blind, but it's still a killer.

Hedgeclipper

If you have a privet hedge, you may find its leaves being devoured by an impressive green caterpillar with purple and white diagonal stripes. This is the caterpillar of the privet hawk-moth, a big moth that lays its eggs on privet leaves.

Although most butterflies and moths are choosy about where they lay their eggs, the privet hawk-moth is lucky because its favorite food plant makes an excellent hedge. The hedge may not be quite so excellent after the caterpillars have been at it, though!

Low profile

Most insects in the bushes try to make themselves hard to see, but the real masters of this art are stick insects and leaf insects. These amazing creatures are so well camouflaged that they look like part of the vegetation.

During daylight they stay very still, hoping to avoid hungry birds. They feed at night, moving very slowly. It's strange to see one leaf being eaten by another, or a green shoot being devoured by a stick. It's lucky they manage to avoid eating each other!

Privet hawk-moth caterpillars like to veg out on a good hedge.

Leafcutter bee

You may see a small bee slicing neat oval sections out of rose leaves with her scissor jaws. Since bees drink nectar, what is a bee doing eating leaves?

Watch closely and you'll see that she doesn't eat them. She carries the leaf sections away to her burrow, rolls them into neat cylinders, and stuffs each one with nectar and pollen. Then she lays an egg in the cylinder and seals it up. Eventually she fills the burrow with these leaf cells. When they hatch, the grubs feed on the nectar and pollen, and emerge as adults the following year.

Leaf-cutter bees can spend all day cutting up plants for use in their burrows.

Evening chorus

Bushes and shrubs often harbor handsome relatives of the grasshopper called bush crickets. Slow-moving and less likely to hop, they are often a beautiful emerald green with extra-long antennae or "feelers". The female has a blade-like ovipositor on her tail that she uses for inserting eggs into crevices. It looks alarming, but it's quite harmless.

Sticky stuff
- Some stick insects breed without mating. The unfertilized eggs all hatch as females. After a while, males can get very scarce, and may even disappear.
- One Asian species of stick insect grows to over 13 inches (33 cm) long, making it the world's longest insect.

BUG ALERT!

The wicked-looking sword on the tail of this bush cricket is simply for laying eggs.

Sapsuckers

Some insects live by sucking the sugary sap from the stems of plants. They are "true bugs", with sharp tubular mouthparts that they use like hypodermic needles. They include greenfly and the broad-bodied shield bugs. Many of these defend themselves with smelly fluids from special glands, so they are sometimes known as *stink bugs*.

The most extraordinary sapsuckers are cicadas. In the warmer parts of the world, male cicadas fill the night air with chirping, buzzing and whistling songs, which they produce using two thin plates on their sides called tymbals. By rattling the tymbals back and forth at high speed, the cicada produces a stream of clicks that sounds like a buzz or chirp.

Song for the asking – cicadas will sing whether you like it or not!

Assassins

Not all bugs are sapsuckers. Some are voracious predators known as assassin bugs. They stalk through the foliage in search of prey, and some lurk in flowers waiting to ambush bees and other visitors.

When an assassin catches something, it uses its needle-sharp beak to skewer it and inject paralyzing nerve poisons. These are mixed with digestive juices that immediately start liquefying its victim's flesh inside its tough outer skin. The bug sucks the flesh through its beak like a milkshake. By the time it has finished slurping every last drop, its luckless victim is just an empty shell.

Cicada data

● A cicada spends most of its life underground as a nymph, and sings only in the last few weeks of its life.

● Each cicada species has a different song so the male attracts the right female.

● The American periodical cicada stays in the ground for up to 17 years. All the cicadas in a certain area emerge in the same year, lay their eggs and then vanish again.

Silken snares

The most conspicuous killers in the bushes are the orb-web spiders that weave their snares across the flyways of their insect prey. Each web is a spiral of sticky silk tacked to radial spokes of non-sticky silk. Often the spider sits at the hub of its web, but if it feels a little exposed, it may seek shelter behind a nearby leaf, holding a single silk thread leading to the web's center.

At the slightest twitch, the spider scurries down the line, pauses briefly to feel the vibe, and then strikes. It is all done by feel because the spider is almost blind. When it contacts the struggling insect the spider bites it to inject paralyzing venom, wraps it in thick silk, and settles to feed.

Running jump

As an assassin bug stalks around one side of a bush, a lynx spider patrols the other. Lynx spiders are hunters that leap on their prey like cats. They have good eyesight, and many species can pinpoint prey from a distance. They jump from leaf to leaf until they are close enough to pounce.

Some lynx spiders have emerald-green bodies, disguising them so well against leaves that they can just sit and wait. They are agile enough to leap at flying insects (even dragonflies), lug them into the bushes, and kill them.

An *Argiope* spider weaves a cross so it doesn't get cross when a bird flies through its web.

Web warning

The most spectacular orb-web spiders are the big, striped, *Argiope* spiders found in warm countries. They weave zigzags of fluffy white silk in the middle of their webs, often in the pattern of a cross. Spiders that make their webs high up in bushes often do this.

It seems that the white cross is a warning to birds, but insect prey seem not to notice. After all, if a bird flies into an *Argiope* web, the spider is left with a big repair job! A special warning sign stops this.

Stretch wrap

Some spiders have come up with amazing ways of using silk to catch prey. One of the most ingenious is the tropical gladiator spider, which lurks near the ground. It has huge eyes, used to locate its victims at night.

The gladiator's weapon is its net – a tiny web no bigger than a postage stamp. It is woven from elastic silk, so by gripping the corners in its front legs, the spider can stretch it out wide. It hangs upside-down from a scaffold of silken threads, holding the net. When a victim appears, the spider suddenly extends all its legs at once, shooting down to stretch the net over its target and snare the insect in a tangle of silk. Then, one quick shot of poison and it's all over.

A gladiator spider widens its net in hungry anticipation.

The bolas spider loves to fish for moths.

Fatal attraction

When it comes to sneaky spider tactics, the prize must go to the bolas spider. This tropical hunter catches flying moths by plucking them out of the night air with a ball of glue on the end of a silken thread. It whirls the ball around with one leg so it sticks to a moth, then reels it in like a fish.

What's most interesting is how the spider lures the moths to its trap. It releases a chemical called a pheromone, which mimics the scent released by female moths when they are ready to mate. Eager male moths are attracted from all over, and the spider simply waits until one flies by. How mean is that?

Stripy snails

Bushes are often full of small snails with attractively banded shells. They feed near the ground but shelter in the bushes. There are two species – one has a white lip on its shell, the other has a brown lip. They are so different in color that you could easily collect six or seven different empty shells in a few minutes.

Every banded snail has its own custom color scheme.

Behind closed doors

Some of the most fascinating spiders hide underground. These are called trapdoor spiders, found in the warmer parts of the world. Each spider builds a silk-lined tunnel with a hinged trapdoor at the entrance. The trapdoor fits like a cork in a bottle. During the day, the spider clings to the underside of the door, holding it shut against spider-hunting wasps. But at night, it partly raises the door and peers out, waiting. When something edible wanders within range, the spider surges forward, stabs it with its poison fangs, and drags it back into the burrow. The door slams shut, and the spider can enjoy its meal in private.

Flip back the lid of a trapdoor spider's burrow and you could get a nasty surprise.

Arachnofax

- One American bolas spider has the scientific name *Mastophora dizzydeani*, after the legendary baseball player Jerome "Dizzy" Dean.
- The huge receptor cells in the gladiator spider's eyes can absorb 2,000 times more light, per cell, than those of spiders that hunt during the day.
- A lynx spider can spray venom like a spitting cobra – so if you find one, don't upset it!

A lynx spider – one spit from this tiny monster and you could be feeling ill.

What's Sitting on the Wall?

An outdoor wall can attract all kinds of small creatures. Old walls are full of holes that make dry refuges for spiders, scorpions, wasps, bees, and lizards. Sunlit walls also warm up like storage heaters during the day, so they are ideal perches for animals that enjoy sunbathing.

Many flying insects rely on the sun's energy to keep them going, and like to rest with their wings angled towards the sun like solar panels. After they have recharged their batteries, they take off and go about their business – provided the spiders, scorpions, and lizards don't get to them first.

Basking flies

Among the most enthusiastic sunbathers are flies. Many are drab, but a few are dazzlingly beautiful. The iridescent metallic sheen of a greenbottle, for example, is so marvelous that you can almost forget it was once a maggot munching dead flesh.

If you live near a farm, your wall may be visited by horseflies with astonishing patterns of green, red and purple on their big compound eyes. These patterns are caused by the scattering of reflected light from the thousands of lenses in each eye. But watch out – these flies are bloodsuckers, and they might take a bite out of you!

The ruby-tailed cuckoo wasp has a stunningly-colored body – it almost looks like a flying jewel.

26

Eyeballed

As basking insects catch the sun's rays, they risk attracting the interest of the stocky, short-legged zebra spider; a spider no bigger than your little fingernail. It is one of the jumping spiders – wickedly effective hunters that specialize in stalking and then jumping on their prey. A jumping spider can leap up to 20 times its own body length and land smack on target, thanks to its excellent eyesight.

You only need to look at a jumping spider to realize how well it can see, because you will find it gazing straight back at you with four big eyes that look like car headlights. The outer pair of eyes are sensitive to movement. When they see you, the spider swivels around to see you with the much bigger inner pair of eyes that work like binoculars. You can't help wondering what it's thinking.

This tropical jumping spider from the Philippines is one of over 4,000 jumping spider species.

Living jewels

Some of the creatures that settle on walls are exquisite. Take the cuckoo wasps. These fast-flying, heat-loving insects blaze with metallic greens, blues and reds, as if cut by a master jeweler. When they get warm, they fly off to find pollen, so you may see them glinting among flowers.

Scuttling scorpions

Peer behind the flaking plaster of an old garden wall in the Mediterranean, and you may come face to face with a little black scorpion. Be careful! It may be small, but it has a nasty sting in its tail and will flourish its sting and lobster claws in warning.

Scorpions are related to spiders, but they carry poison in their tails, not their fangs. Most of the time a scorpion does not bother to sting its prey, because it can kill insects with its pincers. The sting comes in useful if it is attacked by bigger animals – including you!

BUG ALERT!

What Lives in the Vegetable Patch?

There's nothing like the taste of home grown vegetables. You may not agree, but that's certainly the opinion of a whole army of hungry aphids, caterpillars, slugs, and other pests that swarm all over the vegetable garden. Planting so many juicy meals close together makes it particularly easy for them, and the more they eat, the faster they breed.

Many gardeners scatter pesticides that can kill birds and mammals as well as pests. They probably don't do humans any good either. But if there is no poison around, the pests are often attacked by other creatures. The resulting maneuvers can be intriguing to watch, so look closely – it's a war zone out there!

Voracious predators

Aphids make tasty prey for predatory insects. Some of the most voracious are the hungry young of ladybirds, lacewings, and hoverflies, which fall upon the aphids like wolves. Each insect devours over 20 aphids per day. The adult ladybirds and lacewings join the feast and, just like the pests, the more they eat, the faster they breed. Before long, aphid swarms are annihilated, and the ladybirds and their allies have to try their luck elsewhere.

An aphid makes a juicy meal for this ladybird.

Aphid plagues

Some of the most annoying pests are also among the smallest – tiny aphids, such as greenfly and blackfly. There are many different kinds, and they all live on the sugary sap of plants. They cluster on a tender green stem, stab their tubular beaks into its veins, and suck. They can carry viral diseases in their saliva. These infections can turn a healthy green plant into a yellowing, blotchy mess, so aphids are a big problem.

A taste of honey

The sap that aphids feed upon is mostly sugary water with a little protein. Aphids need protein to grow, so they have to eat a lot of sap to get enough protein. This means swallowing far more sugar than they need. They get rid of the surplus sugar by squirting it out of their back ends as honeydew. Ants love honeydew and, being ants, they are very well organized, so they have become honeydew farmers.

Black garden ants herd the aphids and "milk" them for honeydew. They defend the aphids from predators, rounding them up and herding them into specially made shelters, where they are protected from enemies. Most amazingly, the ants gather aphid eggs in late summer and carry them back to their nest, where they stay safe until they hatch in spring.

Sweet, sugary plant sap is food and drink to this hungry young rose aphid.

29

Production line

Aphids multiply rapidly. At the end of summer, male and female aphids mate and produce frost-proof winter eggs. In spring the eggs hatch, but all the young aphids are females who can give birth to their young without mating first. When they find a good food source, each female gives birth to several young every day.

All these young are female, too, and produce their own young within about two weeks. Soon, the garden is overrun. Then, as summer fades, a generation of males is born. These mate with females to produce winter eggs, and the cycle starts over again.

Springbugs

Sometimes you'll find cabbages or other plants peppered with holes. Look closer and you may see tiny, shiny flea beetles. The reason for their name soon becomes obvious because, as you approach, they leap in all directions like fleas. They hide until you go away, and then sneak back to their meal.

Criminal damage

BUG ALERT!

Ladybirds are good news in the garden, but a similar beetle is one of the most notorious insect pests of all. The Colorado beetle is a little yellow and black striped beetle first discovered in Colorado in 1824. It was feeding on the leaves of buffalo burr, a wild relative of the potato plant, until farmers settled on the land and started planting potatoes. The beetles discovered a new food, and 50 years later they had eaten their way right across America, stripping potato plants of every scrap of foliage. They are so destructive that, in some countries, you should inform the police if you see one!

The Colorado beetle (and larva) comes from the wild, wild west.

Is it edible? A great gray slug investigates a possible meal.

Slugs 'n' snails

If you visit the vegetable patch on a wet night, you can hear a steady, low munching. Shine a flashlight and there they are – slugs and snails, plowing their way through leaves and tender stems, leaving silvery trails as evidence of their crimes. Gardeners hate them because they can wipe out whole crops in one night. It can be very discouraging.

There is a good reason why slugs and snails are so destructive – most animals have trouble digesting the cellulose fiber that plants use to build their stems and leaves. This tough, woody material is actually made of sugar, but the sugar is bound together in such a way that normal digestive juices cannot get at it. Slugs and snails are unusual because they can turn cellulose into sugar. For a slug, a green leaf is as sweet as a peach.

Gas attack

Cabbages attract all sorts of insects. The most obvious are the caterpillars of the cabbage white butterflies that flutter around the cabbage crop all summer. The butterflies lay so many eggs on cabbages that the teeming caterpillars reduce the vegetables to skeletons.

While they feed, the caterpillars of large white butterflies absorb the mustard oils from cabbage leaves, concentrating them into a foul-smelling poison. It is the same substance as the mustard gas used as a weapon during World War I. Not surprisingly, birds tend to leave them alone.

What's Burrowing through the Soil?

It may be just dirt to you, but to many small animals the soil is home. There's plenty to eat, provided it is rich in the decaying remains of plants and animals. These feed microscopic organisms, like fungi and bacteria, which turn them into vital chemicals that plants absorb through their roots. A fertile soil is full of living things that feed animals like earthworms. These are eaten by moles, foxes – and, of course, early birds.

Earthworms just can't eat enough dirt – they love it!

Wonderworms

Some soils are sweet, crumbly and fertile. This is almost entirely due to earthworms. These boneless, blind, slimy creatures spend their lives burrowing through the soil and eating it. They crunch it up in their muscular gizzards, digest the edible fragments, and eject the rest, sometimes at the surface as coiled wormcasts.

Earthworms move mountains of soil every day, churning it up, bringing plant foods to the surface, and allowing air in through their tunnels. Without worms, the soil becomes airless, stale and dead.

Earthworm extras

- On wet nights, earthworms emerge from their tunnels to look for food. They keep their tails in their holes so they can retreat from their enemies.
- In southern Africa and Australia, there are monster earthworms over 10 feet (3 meters) long!
- Anything left on the ground long enough is buried by soil which is brought to the surface by earthworms.

Wormkillers

Earthworms have many enemies – birds, badgers and foxes snap them up with relish – but there are more secretive killers in the soil itself. They include the shelled slug *Testacella*, which feeds on earthworms and other slugs, harpooning them with its barbed tongue.

Another worm killer is the New Zealand flatworm, a voracious creature that reaches many parts of the world in potted plants. These flatworms can wipe out whole populations of earthworms, with disastrous consequences for the soil.

Cluster flies, furry relatives of the housefly, lay eggs on earthworms. When the fly maggots hatch, they eat the worms alive.

Gravedigger

If a cat kills a mouse in the yard, the corpse soon disappears. A scavenging bird may eat it, or it may be buried by the extraordinary sexton beetle.

These beetles bury small, dead animals as food for their young. Together, the male and female dig away beneath a body so it sinks into the soil. They skin it and fold it into a tight ball, and then the female lays her eggs. Five days later, the beetle grubs hatch, and their mother helps feed them. Soon they have eaten the whole mouse, and are ready to turn into adults themselves.

Underground acrobats

A shovelful of soil is likely to contain wriggling, multi-legged centipedes. Soil-living centipedes have amazingly flexible, armored bodies. If a centipede arrives at a dead-end in a soil cavity, it just doubles back and crawls out, passing the rest of its long body still coming in. Like other centipedes they are hunters, killing insects, spiders, and worms with their poison fangs.

Sexton beetles really like to eat out, dining on the insides of small, dead animals.

What Lives in the Pond?

Nothing attracts wildlife like a pond. Natural ponds teem with life, and even a brand new manmade pond attracts all kinds of creatures. Add a few water plants and rocks for the animals to hide among, and you have an instant nature reserve. If you can resist the temptation to fill it with fish – they eat everything – you'll be amazed by what moves in.

The most obvious tenants are frogs. In early spring they gather in force, leaving masses of frogspawn that hatch into tadpoles. Some of these may be eaten by the ferocious aquatic young of dragonflies who live for a year or more at the bottom of the pond. The pond surface provides a hunting ground for insects that can somehow walk on the water without sinking. It's fascinating to watch, but don't fall in.

This emperor dragonfly has just emerged from its nymph skin.

Air strike

The most spectacular visitors to a garden pond arrive by air – glittering, brightly-colored dragonflies. The bigger ones zoom towards you like helicopters, but they have huge eyes and excellent vision, and always swerve to avoid you. Other insects are not so lucky, as dragonflies are ferocious killers. They snatch their victims out of the air and carry them to a perch to eat.

There are two main types of dragonfly. The big, fast-flying ones settle with their wings outspread; smaller, fluttery ones called damselflies fold their wings along their bodies. Damselflies look delicate, but they are good hunters too.

Killer nymphs

Female dragonflies lay their eggs in water – some just scattering from the air, others laying them carefully on pondweed. They must mate first, though, and you can often see them sitting on leaves locked in their heart-shaped mating embrace. Some fly in tandem while the female lays her eggs – the male clinging to her neck with his tail.

The eggs hatch as drab, wingless nymphs that live underwater. They have long legs, good eyesight, and murderously efficient extendible jaws. Creeping slowly across the bottom of the pond, a nymph stalks a tadpole or similar victim and suddenly shoots out its jaws like a mechanical grab. It happens faster than the eye can see – certainly too fast for the luckless tadpole.

Dragonflies have never breathed fire, but they look like they might!

Magical transformation

A dragonfly nymph is a nasty, creepy creature, but it magically transforms into an adult dragonfly. It crawls out of the water and clings to a plant stem. After a while, its skin splits and a pale, crumpled, stumpy-looking animal hauls itself out.

At first, this doesn't look remotely like a dragonfly, but gradually it pumps its body and wings up to their full size. As they harden in the sun, the metallic colors start to glow. Eventually, hours after the drab nymph first emerges, the glittering dragonfly soars up and away, leaving its old, empty self clinging to the stem.

Dragon facts

- Dragonflies are among the most ancient of flying insects. Fossil remains of huge dragonflies with wingspans of up to 2½ ft (75 cm) have been found in rocks formed over 300 million years ago – before dinosaurs existed!
- Dragonflies are among the fastest of all flying insects, able to fly at speeds of up to 35 mph (56 km/h).
- Each eye of a big dragonfly contains up to 30,000 lenses, and it has virtually all-around vision.

Portable palaces

In the bottom of the pond, you may see creatures that look like tiny stone walls lumbering about. They are caddis fly larvae, which build themselves protective cases from pieces of stone or leaf – or anything they can find in the pond. They glue the fragments together and live inside them until they are ready to turn into adults. Captive caddis larvae can be persuaded to use miniature shells, pieces of colored glass, or even precious stones with dazzling results.

Aqualung

If you're lucky, your garden pond may attract a water spider. This amazing creature lives entirely underwater, but like all spiders it has to breathe air. It survives by carrying its own air supply in a silvery bubble around its body, like the original aqualung.

It even makes underwater air stores by trapping air bubbles in bell-shaped webs attached to water weed. The spider uses these diving bells as refuges when it wants to feed, and the female raises her babies in them.

Water spiders carry their own scuba diving gear.

36

The great diving beetle looks for its next fish dinner.

Water tigers

The water spider's aqualung technique is also used by the great diving beetle. This hunter chases prey as large as small fish, driving itself through the water with its paddle-like back legs. It carries an air supply under its hinged wing-cases, returning to the surface to top it up.

Diving beetle larvae are known as water tigers. They seize their victims in huge, curved fangs, and inject powerful digestive fluids. These turn their victim's insides into slush, which is then sucked up through the killer's fangs. Delicious!

Walking on water

To us, the surface of a pond is something you fall through, but to many small insects it is a home. The molecules of water at the surface cling together to form an elastic film called surface tension, which is strong enough to support insects if their feet have special water-resistant pads.

These water-walkers include the pond skater, a slender bug that attacks flying insects that crash-land in the water. Attracted by the ripples, it stabs the struggling insects and sucks them dry.

The little water boatman looks very like a backswimmer, but prefers life the right way up.

Bugs a-plenty

One of the strangest hunters in the pond is the backswimmer. This curious little bug spends its life swimming on its back or hanging upside-down beneath the surface film, watching for prey. When it sees a likely victim, it dives in pursuit, rowing itself along with its long back legs, and then stabs it. It can stab you too, so watch out!

Predatory bugs are particularly good at living on or in the water. Another one is the ferocious water scorpion. This bug grabs victims with its front legs like an aquatic praying mantis. It breathes air through a long snorkel tube extending from its tail. The tube may look like a sting, but it's the other end you have to avoid!

What's Hiding in the Woodpile?

A stack of firewood or rocks can make a perfect home for all kinds of creatures. The spaces between the logs or stones are sheltered and dry, like natural rock crevices or hollow trees. As long as the stack stays undisturbed, many animals can spend their whole adult lives in it.

Some animals live in timber or under bark. Many insect grubs tunnel through the wood of growing or dead trees, and when the timber is sawn and stacked, they continue feeding inside the logs. Eventually they may hatch as adult beetles, moths or wasps, but many never get the chance. Even if they emerge, they are likely to be pounced upon by lurking spiders, centipedes, or scorpions. Some of these can be deadly to people too, so if you're rooting in the woodpile, be *very* careful!

Bark beetle galleries make nice patterns, but may destroy the tree.

Tree killers

If the bark falls off an old log, you may see the radiating galleries of bark beetle grubs. The adult beetles lay their eggs under the bark, and when the eggs hatch the tiny grubs start eating their way out from the egg chamber. As they eat they grow, so their burrows get wider too. Eventually they turn into beetles and gnaw their way out.

The beetle grubs can eat the wood because they carry a fungus that digests wood fiber. But this causes Dutch elm disease, which has destroyed huge numbers of elm trees in Europe and North America. So if the logs in your woodpile are cut from dead elms, you may see the evidence.

Wood processor

While small insects burrow beneath the bark, bigger ones bore through the timber. They are the grubs of wood wasps and longhorn beetles. Like bark beetles, they may carry fungi that make wood digestible, but they also have strong gnawing jaws.

They live for years in the timber, then emerge from large holes as winged adults. Some of these are impressive beasts. Female wood wasps, in particular, have long egg-laying tubes – ovipositors – for drilling into timber. They look like wickedly powerful stings, but they're harmless.

Airborne

An old log makes a snug refuge for the click beetle, which can hurl itself into the air with a loud click. It squeezes the front and rear parts of its body together with a set of powerful muscles until a special catch clicks shut, flicking both ends of its body against the ground to catapult it into the air. Whee!

Click beetles are real gymnasts.

The bionic drill of the ichneumon wasp is tipped with metal for maximum bite.

Deadly drill

You would think that an insect grub burrowing through solid timber would be safe from attack by other insects, but it isn't. The delicate-looking ichneumon wasp is looking for somewhere to lay her eggs. She has a long, slender ovipositor, with a sharp drill tip that is hardened with metals such as manganese and zinc. She drills her way into the grub's timber tunnel, lays an egg and flies off.

When the egg hatches, the ichneumon larva latches onto the burrowing grub and starts eating it alive. Meanwhile, the grub keeps eating, converting wood into flesh to feed the ichneumon. This is a thankless task, as the ichneumon larva eventually kills the grub anyway.

Chink in the armor

The most numerous creatures in the woodpile are likely to be woodlice, feeding on rotting wood. These small, armored creatures are crustaceans, like shrimps, crabs and lobsters. Most crustaceans live in water and breathe through gills, but the woodlouse manages to survive on land by carrying a supply of water around in its damp gills. If it dries out it suffocates, so it always hides in damp places.

Woodlice are often attacked and eaten by centipedes, which stab them with their curved poison fangs. But their main enemy is a six-eyed spider with brick-red legs that has made woodlouse-killing its profession. Equipped with extra-long fangs like curved needles, the woodlouse spider seizes its victim with one fang piercing its back and the other piercing its belly. It injects a deadly shot of venom, and the woodlouse is history.

Woodlice are actually relatives of crabs.

Probably the most dangerous spider in the world – the Sydney funnelweb!

BUG ALERT!

Pickaxe fangs

In southeastern Australia, there could be something very nasty hiding in a log pile.

The Sydney funnelweb spider is one of the world's most venomous spiders. Big, black, and shiny with huge pickaxe fangs, it usually hides in a silken tunnel that flares out into a funnel-shaped sheet of threads. These work like tripwires so that when an animal snags its foot on a wire, the spider rushes out, grabs and stabs it. As the poison gets to work, the spider drags its victim back into its lair and eats it.

The biggest, nastiest-looking funnelwebs are female, but for some reason the male's venom is much more dangerous, containing nerve poisons that can kill you within a few hours. Males are also much more likely to wander away from their burrows than females – they may even turn up inside a house. This is one occasion when being afraid of spiders is definitely sensible!

Red for danger

If you live outside Australia, there's no need to worry about funnelweb spiders. Don't relax just yet, though – there is a deadly spider that lives in many warm countries, and often hides in log piles – the black widow.

As its name suggests, it's the female that does the damage. She has small fangs, but even they are long enough and strong enough to pierce your skin and inject an awesomely powerful nerve poison, estimated to be 15 times stronger than rattlesnake venom. The spider produces it in tiny quantities, but the venom from just one black widow is enough to kill a horse.

Easily distinguished by a bright red mark, black widows are shy, retiring creatures. If they are disturbed, they usually run away and hide. But sometimes they have to defend themselves, and if you are in the way and get bitten you'd better find a doctor – quickly!

The black widow spider – the female of the species definitely wears the trousers.

The black widow is one dark lady you don't want to upset.

Widow bytes

● Black widow spiders live all over the world, but the American black widow is probably the most dangerous.

● Male black widows are tiny creatures, and, although they may be just as poisonous as their sisters, they aren't big enough to bite you.

● In the days when houses had outdoor lavatories, black widow spiders were notorious for lurking there and biting anyone who disturbed them. Nasty!

● The nerve poison of a black widow causes muscle spasms that can paralyze your breathing, with deadly results. If you can manage to keep breathing, you survive the bite.

What Lives in the Compost Heap?

Many yards have compost heaps: piles of uprooted weeds, soft green leaves, vegetable peelings, and grass clippings. Over time, this rots down into rich crumbly compost – the best fertilizer of all.

A compost heap teems with mostly microscopic life. Millions of tiny organisms are hard at work, attacking the greenery. They generate heat and the whole heap warms up. This makes it an ideal nursery for reptiles like the slow worm, a legless lizard that bears beautiful, copper-colored live young. There are plenty of slugs and insects for the slow worm to eat, and given the chance, it will live in the heap all year round.

Yellow peril

One of the most important animals in the compost heap is the dark red, orange-banded brandling worm. It eats dead plant material and turns it into something that the microscopic organisms can work on. If you disturb it, however, this worm produces a vile-smelling yellow fluid. Eeuuch!

Compost heaps are often alive with juicy worms.

Legwaves

Some animals feasting in the compost heap look like shiny black worms, but you'll see they have legs – a lot of legs. These are millipedes.

The word millipede means "1000 feet," which is a bit of an exaggeration, but most have well over 100. A typical millipede's body is made up of about 60 cylindrical segments, most of which carry two pairs of legs. That makes over 200 in total.

A millipede moves its legs in sequence, so the whole row of legs ripples in a wave. The wave drives it along and all those tiny leg muscles allow it to force its way through stiff soil. Since it dries up quickly in the sun, it soon slips out of sight.

How many legs? A black garden millipede certainly wouldn't be able to afford shoes!

Mighty mollusk

A compost heap is a feast for large black slugs. These mighty mollusks prefer to eat dead, rotting plants, so they are a lot less destructive than smaller garden slugs.

Obviously, a slug cannot retreat into its shell like a snail. But if you upset one of these big slugs, it pulls in its tentacles and contracts its whole body into a hard, round, prune-like lump.

Springloaded

The smallest creatures that you'll see in the compost heap are springtails – tiny gray or brown insects that feed on rotting vegetation. Each springtail has a long springy fork hinged to its back end. The springtail normally holds this clipped beneath its body, but if it is scared, it releases it. The spring flicks down against the ground, throwing the springtail into the air and, hopefully, out of trouble.

Slugs are just snails without shells, but they do pretty well without them.

Quiz Pages

Baffling Bugs

These pictures all show bits of bugs.
Can you name them?

5

4

2

7

1

3

6

8

Animal Anagrams

Try unscrambling these jumbled-up words to find out
which bugs and microbes are lurking on this page.

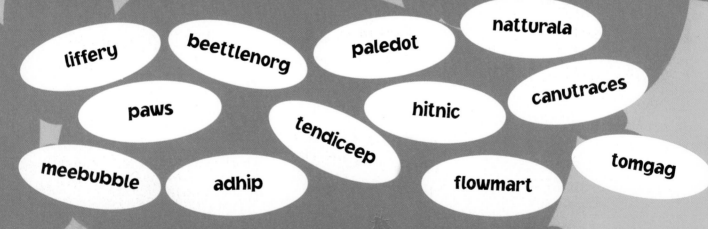

natturala

liffery

beettlenorg

paledot

paws

hitnic

canutraces

tendiceep

meebubble

adhip

flowmart

tomgag

Having a bit of trouble? Are the answers bugging you? See page 46 for some help.

Minibeast Mindbenders

Can you name a creature that:

1   eats dead wood for lunch?
2   has an air-supply bubble for breathing in water?
3   is a small crustacean whose main enemy is a six-eyed spider?
4   can grow to 13 inches (33 cm) long?
5   turns its dinner into a milk shake with paralyzing nerve poison?
6   has a web no bigger than a postage stamp?
7   has a scissor jaw and sucks blood?
8   can turn its head all the way around to face the wrong way?
9   is small, green and a relative of the greenfly?
10 is a cabbage muncher that makes its own deadly mustard gas?

How many did you score?

1-4   It's a good start! Now go back and do some more reading.
5-7   Great! You've certainly learned a lot.
8+   Excellent! You must be the world's expert on what lives in the grass, on the flowers, and even in the vegetable patch!

Nasty Numbers

Can you remember the answers to these nauseating number puzzles?

1 A swarm of locusts can contain up to how many individual insects?
  a 5,000
  b 50,000
  c 5 million
  d 50 billion

2 How fast can dragonflies travel?
  a Up to 10 mph
  b Up to 16 mph
  c Up to 34 mph
  d Up to 41 mph

3 How far away can you hear a cricket's 'song'?
  a Up to 20 yards
  b Up to 500 yards
  c Up to 1 mile
  d Up to 3 miles

4 How long can monster earthworms grow?
  a 1 yard
  b 2 yards
  c 3 yards
  d 4 yards

5 Roughly how many legs does a millipede usually have?
  a Over 100
  b Over 200
  c Over 500
  d Over 1,000

6 What is the legspan of the goliath bird-eating spider?
  a 5 inches
  b 8 inches
  c 11 inches
  d 16 inches

Answers

Nasty Numbers

1 d
2 c
3 c
4 c
5 b
6 c

Minibeast Mindbenders

1 Termite
2 Water spider
3 Woodlouse
4 Stick insect
5 Assassin bug
6 Gladiator spider
7 Blackfly
8 Praying mantis
9 Froghopper
10 Cabbage white butterfly caterpillar

Animal Anagrams

maggot

flatworm

aphid

bumblebee

centipede

chitin

wasp

crustacean

tadpole

greenbottle

firefly

tarantula

Baffling Bugs

1 Bee-fly
2 Orb-web spider
3 Garden spider
4 Ruby-tailed cuckoo wasp
5 Bumblebee
6 Desert locust
7 Black widow spider
8 Tropical jumping spider

46

Index

a

ant, black, 9, 29
  fire, 9
  harvester, 9
  tending aphids, 29
aphid, 4, 28-30
  blackfly, 29
  greenfly, 29
  mating, 30
Argiope sp., 23
assassin bug, 22

b

backswimmer, 37
badger, 33
bark, beetle gallery, 38
bat, eaten, 11
bee, African, 14
  bumblebee, 8, 15
  honey-, 14
  killer, 14
  leafcutter, 21
  mining, 8, 13
bee-fly, 13
beetle, click, 39
  Colorado, 30
  flea, 30
  galleries, 38
  great diving, 37
  lily, 17
  longhorn, 39
  rose chafer, 16
  sexton, 33
  soldier, 16
bird, 32-3

black widow spider, 11
blackfly, 5, 19
blackfly aphid, 29
buddleia, 12
bug, assassin, 22-3
  shield, 22
bumblebee, 8, 15
butterfly, cabbage white, 31
  tortoiseshell, 12

c

caddis fly larvae, 36
caterpillar, 20, 31
cellulose, 31
centipede, 33, 40
chitin, 12
cicada, 22
cricket, bush, 21
  field, 7
  mole, 7
crustacea, 40
cuckoo spit, 17

d

damselfly, 34
digestion, 29, 31, 32
dragonfly, emperor, 34
  nymph, 35

e

earthworm, 32-3
earwig, 17
enzyme, 8

f

firefly, 8
flatworm, New Zealand, 33
fly, bee-fly, 13
  blackfly, 5, 19
  cluster, 33
  greenbottle, 26
  horsefly, 26
  hoverfly, 18, 28
fossil, dragonfly, 35
fox, 33
frog, eaten, 11
  spawn, 34
  tadpole, 34-5
froghopper, 17

g

glow-worm, 8
grasshopper, 6-7
  meadow, 7
greenbottle, 26
greenfly, 17, 29

h

habitat, 4-6
honey-bee, 14
honeydew, 29
honeysuckle, 13
horsefly, 26
hoverfly, 18, 28